READing is more than Phonics !

A Parents' Guide for Reading
with Beginning or Discouraged Readers

Vera Goodman

edited by Terry Davies

READING CIRCLES – Calgary, Alberta, Canada

Publisher: **Reading Circles**
                P.O. Box 33038
                3919 Richmond Road S.W.
                Calgary, Alberta
                Canada T3E 7E2

ISBN 0-9699938-0-3

Canadian Cataloguing in Publication Data

Goodman, Vera Elizabeth, 1934-
   Reading is more than phonics

   Includes bibliographical references.
   ISBN 0-9699938-0-3

   1. Reading – Parent participation.   I. Davies, Terry E. (Terry Elizabeth), 1957-   II. Title.
LB1050.2.G66 1995   649'.58   C95-910818-1

Design:

Gail Pocock, Bulldog Communications
Ste. 3, 830 - 19 Ave. S.W., Calgary, Alberta, Canada T2T 0H5

Printing:

Friesen Printers
Ste. 120, 3016 - 19th St. N.E., Calgary, Alberta, Canada T2E 6Y9

Printed and Bound in Canada

This book is dedicated
to the children and parents
who have been my teachers.

Lisa -

To an old time friend &
rider who is
now teaching others

All the best

Vera

Table of **Contents**

Introduction INTRODUCTION

As a **PARENT** *you have been cast in the* **ROLE** *of your child's most important* **TEACHER**. *The* practice that makes perfect *takes place at* **HOME**.

Dialogue between adult and child is at the heart of successful reading.

Recently a mother phoned to thank me for my influence in her son Robin's life. I tutored Robin in grade two. He is now doing well in grade six and, best of all, he loves to read. In the course of our conversation his mother made a gratifying comment, "I realize now that fifty percent of what you did for Robin was in what you did for me. I was frustrated, worried and anxious. You helped me to relax and enjoy reading with my son. I let him develop at his own pace and it has really paid off."

Academic success is based on the ability to read. To help each of my students reach their potential, I decided early in my teaching career to become knowledgeable and competent in the field of reading instruction. Combining what I had learned from the work of others with my own observations, I set about doing classroom research. Later, as an administrator, I assisted in conducting research projects that proved to be unusually successful with children who were delayed in reading.

Reading can be learned through many different teaching methods. Regardless of how reading is being taught, the relationship between an adult and a child as they practice together has a great impact, not only on learning to read, but on whether the child will choose to read as a pastime. In this book I attempt to give simple, practical ideas that will help parents to make the best use of time spent practicing.

During the past three years I have spent hundreds of hours tutoring individual students and working with their parents. The reading philosophy presented here is based on lessons learned from these interactions and on twenty-seven years of teaching and learning with classes from grades one to nine.

Both parents and educators who know my work have urged me to write this book. It is meant to be a guide that you can read, digest and return to when necessary. I focus my writing on behaviors that affect what happens *today* as you sit beside your child with a book to share. I do not want to present a yardstick by which to measure your past experiences.

No attempt is made to present a reading method or to provide a recipe for success. I simply share beliefs and strategies that have proven successful in my work with students over the years. Many discussions in the book are directed to the parents of children who are having trouble learning to read. I realize that the majority of children learn to read well and are anxious to read with their parents from the start. However, the approach to reading and the activities presented in this book will enrich the sharing time of *all* those who are helping others learn to read.

Some children have learning problems which make reading more difficult. They are in special need of coaching that shows them how to bring all their strengths to reading. It has been my experience that children will read more easily and with greater understanding if they are given strategies that support them in positive ways.

It is not always possible to tutor your own child. Emotions and conflicting expectations can get in the way. For a while, you may need to have your child read to someone else. But don't give up your sharing time. Enjoy books together. When children are ready, they want to read to others.

I have dealt with many frustrated parents. One distraught mother told me she would ask herself, "What am I doing wrong? How am I failing? I've been a bad mother today, I haven't read with my child." It is natural and important to be concerned about your child's progress. I hope that the approach to reading presented in this book will let you relax and have fun learning together.

Currently, the pendulum of public discussion seems to be swinging in the direction of phonics. Phonics instruction is being presented as the simple answer to illiteracy. Although a knowledge of letters and their sounds is important, those who are learning to read need a variety of strategies to use as they approach printed text. They also need positive support to build confidence.

My purpose is to put phonics into perspective. There are many factors that affect one's ability to read. Reading is more than phonics!

"It is not the bookish home, nor necessarily the middle-class family, not high intelligence, good eye movements, acute ears, nor even extensive vocabulary that makes the successful beginner. The supporting adult, who shows him what a book is and how print works, who helps him to discover reading and expects him to be successful, makes all the difference. Together, adult and child learn about reading."

Margaret Meek

Acknowledgements CREDITS

Who do you **ACKNOWLEDGE** *when there are so many who have* **INFLUENCED** *your ideas and your writing?*

Thanks to all the people who have enriched my life.

My success as a teacher has been fostered by years of watching master teachers practice their craft. My view of reading has been framed by studying the research of scholars in the field of literacy.

Margaret Meek, a noted British educator, has greatly influenced my understanding of reading and learning. The reading model in Chapter Two is based on her beliefs about how children learn to read. Listening to Humbarto Maturana, a biologist from Chili, enhanced my understanding of life. This man's ability to simplify the complexities of everyday living enabled me to simplify my view of reading. The diagram in Chapter Three is an adaptation of his behavior model.

Many others have been generous with their support. Several people read my manuscript and gave me valuable feedback. Quotes on the cover are excerpts from letters I have received. Bernie and Jan McCaffery kept urging me to write this book so that other parents could share the insights they found valuable. Marg Edmonds prodded me to get started and encouraged me to keep writing. Rae Sharpe read my rough drafts many times and provided intellectual and emotional support.

The skillful editing of Terry Davies helped to clarify for others what was so obvious to me. Gail Pocock of Bulldog Communications put it all together very professionally.

The patient and loving support of my husband, Don, gave me freedom to write. My grandsons, Sean and Bryce, keep me aware of the responsibility I have to encourage a new generation of readers.

How do Children LEARN?

I *am convinced that the* **EXPERIENCES** *of the child, the* **BEHAVIOURS** *of the family and the* **EXPECTATIONS** *of the society in which they live are all part and parcel of* **LEARNING** *to* **READ**.

Reading goes beyond the printed page in many significant ways.

Reading skills are acquired as we read books, share experiences and engage in talk with children. Feelings, attitudes, beliefs and the climate within the family are all important. Children will pick up the view of reading presented by their first teachers, the family.

Family members who know a child and the experiences which have been part of the child's life are equipped to provide the support their young reader needs. Although it is possible for children to learn to read by reading only at school, most require extra practice.

Reading is learned through apprenticeship. Just as you cannot learn to drive a car by reading a book on how to drive a car, you cannot learn to read by reading a book on how to read. The art of reading is gained through **guided practice.**

How do humans learn? The most obvious ways that come to mind are memorizing, experiencing, practicing and listening. In our society, we often think of learning as being the result of formal education. However, much of what we learn happens without conscious awareness and many more subtle factors are involved.

The brain builds a *pool of knowledge* based on experiences encountered from moment to moment. We cannot stop ourselves from learning. However, what is learned may not be what we want to learn or what is being taught. For instance, it is possible that efforts to teach reading might result in some children learning to dislike reading.

CHILDREN LEARN FROM:

- experiencing success and failure
- being tested and labelled
- copying the behaviours of others
- taking risks and dealing with consequences
- interacting with peers
- listening in on adult conversations
- hearing and telling stories
- interpreting facial expressions and tone of voice
- being rewarded for behaviours
- and so on, and so on...

THE ROLE OF SELF-TALK

Individually, we make sense of experience by talking to ourselves in thought. In our self-talk we make up conversations, relate new ideas to prior experiences, reflect on how our words and actions are received by others and plan future behaviours. It is the way we define who we are and how we view our world. The brain organizes these inputs into *little worlds of experience* which we use to make sense of our lives. We become the person we talk to ourselves about!

The difficulty with self-talk is that it is not necessarily true nor accurate. The comments, motives and attitudes encountered are often interpreted incorrectly as we think, reflect and react. Nevertheless, it all becomes part of the experience base which guides future decision-making and frames our view of life. It is possible for a child to talk himself out of reading!

Self-talk is the way in which children give themselves instructions. They actively create their own learning from the information they receive. The ability to learn effectively is determined by their emotional state and it is self-talk that determines how they feel.

Each family builds its own language of self-talk – talk that helps each individual either to maintain a positive self-image or to build feelings of incompetence and inferiority.

The ability to read well depends on the breadth of our experience. Children are in great need of extended discussion with adults on a variety of subjects. Through such dialogue they learn valuable thinking skills and recognize that they have opinions and ideas that are valued by others. Talking together about current events, history, science and other subjects builds academic confidence. A child cannot talk to himself about important and interesting topics if he has never been exposed to them.

One father I know reads the atlas with his pre-schoolers. He tells stories from various countries and points out interesting things about the physical world. They love it! He is instilling a lifelong interest in geography and history!

What kinds of things do you say in your child's hearing about reading, learning, teachers and school? Comments such as, "Your school library sure has a lot of interesting books we can share," and "You should hear the good story Jennifer can tell to accompany the pictures in this book," build positive images of reading and books. On the other hand, "Jennifer can't read, I don't know what we're going to do!" or, "Don't schools teach reading anymore?" undermine confidence.

A mother who was extremely worried because her seven-year-old son couldn't read yet told me that, out of frustration, she was saying things like, "You can't even read *the*, or *of*, or *from*! Those are baby words!" What a perfect way to reinforce his suspicion that reading is too hard for him!

You may have legitimate concerns about your child's progress or the ways in which she is being taught. Share these concerns with the teacher, not the child. If you discuss your frustrations about her reading with others, make sure she is not listening. Negative remarks have a very negative influence.

Humans seem to have an inborn ability to live up to labels and nicknames. The words you use to describe your child as a reader will have a strong effect on who she will become.

Confidence building is the key to reading success. The trick is to talk positively, to assure children we believe in them until they have had the time and experience to believe in themselves. For young children this involves keeping from them any hint that they might not become skillful readers.

Childhood is a fragile time. Confidence is a flame that can be extinguished by a little puff of doubt. Reading is especially subject to the winds of doubt. It involves risk-taking and beginners must see themselves as successful **before** they are capable. The learner must be invited, from the beginning, to behave like a reader. The kind of self-talk we want to cultivate is, "It's ok. It's a little tough, but I can do it!" I cannot stress too much the importance of maintaining this kind of confidence.

How many words do you have to read to be a reader? ...One! I let my beginners know this. An appropriate comment might be, "Look at that! You can read. If you can read one word, you can read thousands of words. You're a reader!" Children can label themselves *reader* early in life. This helps them to maintain a positive image of themselves as readers.

Attitude has a great influence on learning. Enjoyment and pleasure are transmitted quickly. So are frustration and disappointment. Children are often hard on themselves and can become discouraged easily. The emotional state of both you and your child influences sharing time. Because discouraged readers are often harder to get on track than beginners they, in particular, need your positive support and enthusiasm. Together you must build the confidence needed for successful reading.

Summary of Key POINTS

READING *goes beyond the printed page.* • *Reading is learned through* **GUIDED PRACTICE**. • *There isn't* **TIME** *for enough practice at school.* • *Children learn by* **TALKING** *to themselves.* • **DIALOGUE** *on meaningful topics builds academic confidence.* • *Children can't talk about things they haven't yet* **ENCOUNTERED**. • *Maintaining confidence is the key to reading success.* • *Beginners must see themselves as successful before they are* **CAPABLE**. • *Negative* **REMARKS** *have a very negative influence.* • *Share your* **CONCERNS** *with the teacher - not the child.*

Essentials for LEARNING to Read ...

To learn to read we need **FOUR** *things, all of which are* **INEXPENSIVE** *and readily* **AVAILABLE** *– One who can* **READ** *– One who wants to* **LEARN** *– Time to* **PRACTICE** *– A selection of interesting* **BOOKS**.

It is not necessary to buy costly reading programs.

Those who want to learn to read can do so by reading with experienced readers. They need a constant supply of interesting books, time to engage in conversations about their contents and a reader to teach strategies and help with practice.

Success in reading is directly related to the quality of dialogue engaged in by the reader and the learner. Reading is an active encounter between reader and print. Effective readers spend time mentally making connections and predicting both words and events. Beginners make these connections orally through conversation. Stop and talk about what you are reading. To create *quality dialogue* relate the story to personal experience, predict what will happen or question a point of view. Together you will discover the pleasures of reading. Shared reading time will be warm and special.

This diagram illustrates the concept of *quality dialogue* – the interaction between the experienced reader, the beginning or discouraged reader and the books they share together.

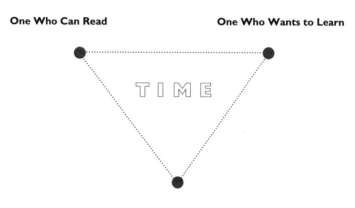

One Who Can Read

One Who Wants to Learn

TIME

A Book Which Interests Them Both

The book is the key to *quality dialogue*. Choosing a book that appeals to the interests of both the experienced reader and the one who is learning will stimulate meaningful discussions.

ONE WHO CAN READ

That's you! Time constraints in schools are such that teachers cannot spend a lot of time reading with individual students. Family members or friends must be prepared to sit beside and help young readers as they practice. Parents can do this well because they know their child's unique interests and experiences. They are also the child's most powerful role model.

The structures and guidelines children need in order to read successfully are taught at school. They are internalized through practicing at home.

Those of us who can read tend to forget that reading is a very personal experience. Society has arbitrarily set six as the age at which all children are expected to learn to read. By organizing children into grades based on age, we have set up an artificial system that expects children to march along as a group. Although everyone knows that this is unrealistic, change is difficult and we continue to put unnecessary pressure on beginners and on their teachers.

Labelling and sorting of students, based on the speed at which they progress in reading, begins in grade one. We foolishly impose standardized reading tests on children who we **already know** can't read independently! What an excellent way to destroy confidence and reinforce despair in those who are not yet ready to read!

Sometimes, as a result, children must repeat the entire year. The first grade child usually can't understand why he is being left behind because he feels he has done his best. And reading gets the blame!

Two stories of children I have known serve to illustrate this point. One little fellow who was not reading by the middle of grade one said to his grandma, "The other kids are away up there and I'm down here and we're getting farther apart. I'm stupid! I hate reading!"

Another boy who was informed that he had to repeat grade one because he hadn't learned to read said to his mother through his tears, "But they didn't teach me!" Both boys are bright and obviously they had both been taught along with the others. They both felt they were doing their best.

Not every seed produces a flower in the same number of days nor does every child learn to read independently on the same schedule. Why can't we accept this and let everyone produce flowers in their own time? We accept it for walking and talking so why should reading be any different? As we teach, support and encourage a beginner we must also trust him to set his own pace. This may be difficult to do when children are tested and labelled too early.

Let's hope that someone doesn't come up with a magic age at which infants must walk and talk or we will have to set up schools for remedial walking and talking!

Until a child has achieved some fluency in reading, it will be difficult to read alone and he should not be asked to do so. It is like learning to walk. We must be prepared to hold a child's hand until he signals that he's ready to try it alone by pulling his hand away - no matter how long that takes!

Letting children learn at their own pace does not mean forsaking standards and expectations. As reading processes are taught and reinforced, children must be challenged to improve their performance. The role of the teacher is to teach the skills needed for reading, to provide new experiences and to monitor progress.

Your most important contribution as a parent is to provide a warm supportive atmosphere, time for sharing, lots of patience and a supply of appropriate books.

ONE WHO WANTS TO LEARN

No one really knows why reading comes so easily to some children while for others progress is slow. What we do know is that every child who enters grade one not only **wants** to learn to read but **expects** to do so. If they do not see themselves as readers fairly quickly, children can get turned off before they have given themselves a chance. They may say to themselves, "I don't want to read! I hate reading! I'm dumb!"

How do children judge their own progress? They might very well compare themselves to the best readers in the class. In many first-grade classes there are children who begin the year already reading independently. There are others who learn to read quickly and are able to join the ranks of those who are members of an exclusive club, *The Club of Readers.*

Those who are not yet reading want very much to belong to *The Club.* In spite of what they say, all children want to read. Fear that they will never be able to master what others seem to be doing so easily leads to discouragement. Young children lack the maturity to realize their uniqueness. Moreover, everyone around them is expecting them to read.

The next step for some children is to avoid reading except when required to do so. They especially don't want to fail before family members, so they are reluctant to read at home. But reading and hockey have a lot in common - if you don't attend the practices you are not likely to make the team!

Books and reading must be seen to be both **pleasurable** and **attainable** or the learner will become discouraged. A discouraged child may not want to spend the time with books that is needed for mastery. Children must find in books human experiences with which they can identify. Don't tell a young child how important reading is, just help him to discover how interesting it can be.

Whether or not a child becomes an independent reader in grade one **is not** important. The image that he builds of himself as a reader and learner **is** important.

TIME

Time is the coin we have to spend. Both the reader and the learner must agree to spend time together. As we deal with the stresses in our busy lives, time is a most difficult thing to find.

When you have a young child who is not yet reading independently, plan both your own and your child's activities so that you have blocks of time for leisurely exploring books together. Keep extracurricular activities to a minimum for a while. Too much activity means that reading has to be squeezed in, often when everyone is overtired.

How we choose to spend our time sends a powerful message about what we value. My experience with Troy's family serves as an example. Both mom and dad worked, so time to spend together was at a premium. Reading was done as homework, sandwiched between baseball, swimming and a host of other activities. Mom assumed responsibility for reading with Troy. Dad taught him hobbies and helped him to achieve success in athletic events.

Troy was often tired when he came to read with me. He said he didn't like reading. Dad and mom assured me that they thought learning to read was important. I'm not sure that the way they were using their time gave that message to Troy!

The family planned together and rearranged their days. Dad and Troy made time to share books and magazines about baseball and other common interests. They began to enjoy learning together. They even found new ways to improve Troy's athletic skills through the books they read! As mom and dad shared different kinds of reading material with Troy his *pool of knowledge* was greatly enriched. It took time, but he is now a successful reader.

The world will not come to an end if you don't read every day. When it comes to reading time, quality is more important than quantity. Short sessions that inspire warm feelings towards books and reading can be balanced off with longer stretches that are more challenging. Relaxed sharing is the goal.

BOOKS

The books you choose to share will make all the difference. Select books on subjects that both you and your young reader enjoy. Interesting books make for an interested reader! I have actually heard people say, "It doesn't matter what children read as long as they are reading." This makes as much sense as saying, "It doesn't matter what children eat as long as they are eating!"

The reading material chosen is *so important* that I have reserved a separate section for its consideration. In Chapter Seven we will look at **why** the choice of book influences the reading process and **how** to choose reading material that is appropriate for your child.

Summary of Key POINTS

Children **WANT** *to read and* **EXPECT** *to learn.*

• *Fear of failure undermines* **CONFIDENCE**. •

Sharing times should be both **FUN** *and*

CHALLENGING. • *Stop and* **TALK** *together as*

you read. • *Don't ask children to read aloud*

to others until they feel **COMFORTABLE**. •

CULTIVATE *your child's interest and your*

flower will bloom in its own time. • *Have*

patience, but continue to actively tend your

reader with **GOOD TEACHING**.

Phonics and EXPERIENCE

Building a **BRIDGE** *between the written word and the reader's unique* **EXPERIENCE** *is essential for* **READING.**

Reading is the result of blending print with experience.

To read, we must have a printed text. This can take many different forms such as words, sentences, pictures, charts and diagrams.

Experience, housed invisibly in the mind, is what the individual reader brings to print. Experience encompasses the information that can be recalled consciously as well as all the beliefs, attitudes and understandings in our subconscious *pool of knowledge.*

Phonics is the study of sounds and letters and how they relate to each other to make words. It is an important part of being able to read words in printed text. For many, phonics is considered to be the most important part of learning to read. Phonics programs are easy to teach and phonics knowledge is easy to test. It may appear logical that if one knows the sounds of letters and their combinations, reading will be easy.

My experience tells me that this is not necessarily true. I tutor students who have been exposed to heavy doses of instruction in phonics and it has made them slow, ineffective readers.

We hear a lot today about going *back to the basics* or getting back to *the good old days* ...whenever they were! As I talk with some who advocate this journey into the past, I find they are referring mainly to teaching reading through phonics.

"Well, I learned to read through phonics," some will say to me. Or, "I didn't learn to read well because they were using the sight method."

"You mean you sat in grade one and kept track of all the ways in which you were being taught to read?" I ask.

"Well, of course I couldn't do that!" they respond, realizing how difficult this would be.

"Then maybe you don't remember all the things that influenced your development as a reader," I conclude.

I decided to look through old Readers and Teaching Guides to discover for myself what the *basics* might have been in the *good old days*. In the Alberta Program of Studies for 1942, I found this interesting advice to teachers:

"Please teacher, don't teach the beginner to read by the phonics method. This method is long out-of-date. It is based on the idea that in reading, the reader moves his eyes from one letter to the next, sounding out the word. A good reader does not move his eyes in this way and no child should have this bad habit fixed upon him. It makes his reading slower in speed and poorer in comprehension."

Recently, I had the good fortune to be reunited with the teacher who taught me to read and who instilled in me a lifelong love of learning. To me, Margaret Elliott was an angel in disguise when she came to our small town in southern Saskatchewan fresh from Normal School. For over 50 years I have treasured her in my thoughts. It was a dream come true to meet her again after all these years. Grade one teachers are special!

My curiosity about how reading was taught in the past prompted me to ask her what reading method she used in teaching us to read. She replied, "We were trained to teach you to read in whole words and sentences but not to break the words up into little parts!" It seems that in *those* good old days phonics was not the first step in learning to read!

This diagram simplifies the relationship of Print to Experience.

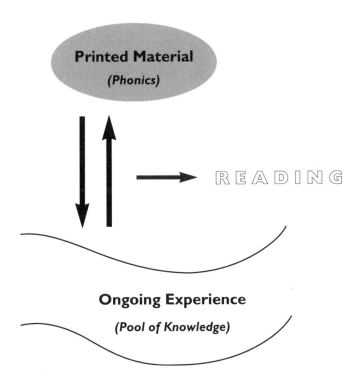

There should be no conflict between the roles of phonics and experience. Without a knowledge of letters, reading is impossible. If phonics training was not important, we would all be able to read solely on the basis of experience. It is equally clear that without experience it is impossible to read with understanding. Making sense out of print is what reading is all about.

One thing has become evident to me over the years. A reader needs to develop a feel for the reading experience before he begins to concentrate his efforts on decoding individual words. Many of the problem readers that I have worked with have the same definition of reading – *sounding out words*. When they view reading in this way their focus is on letters and individual words. There are many ways to approach reading, but readers who are intent on sounding out are often unable to take advantage of other strategies. They may even be unaware of them. Attention must be shifted to the meaning. **Reading is making sense of print.**

Children must utilize all their capabilities while reading. They must be made to realize how much they already know that can help them to read. We need to show a child how to use his own *pool of knowledge* to unlock the mystery of print.

I am concerned when children label themselves by saying, "I have dyslexia," or some other *learning disorder*. If they feel they have a condition that is beyond their control, children can lose confidence in their own abilities. By taking on such a label, children may feel unable to learn by themselves and look to someone else to *rescue* them. Reading takes place in each child's mind. No one else can do it for them.

I find that once a child has assumed a label, it is difficult to develop the confidence he needs to read alone. Learning difficulties should be discussed among parents, teachers and specialists. Together they can plan appropriate strategies that will enable the child to rediscover the joy of learning. Children do not need to know the labels.

Many of the parents I talk to have one phrase they use most often as they help their children practice: *Sound it out!* This reflects an emphasis solely on phonics and does not suggest any other approaches. Efficient readers must use strategies that go beyond phonics. Successful reading is finding a **happy balance** between phonics and experience. The purpose of this book is to help you find that balance. The next chapter contains activities that demonstrate more clearly how readers can use their experience to make sense of the printed word.

Summary **of** **K**ey **Points**

There is more to reading than **PHONICS**. •
Reading is **BLENDING** print with experience.
• There should be no conflict between the
ROLES of phonics and experience in reading. •
When we give children a **LABEL** they may live up
to it. • We must help children to **RECOGNIZE** and
use all their capabilities as they read. • Making
sense of **PRINT** is what reading is all about.

Reading with UNDERSTANDING

Bringing **EXPERIENCE** *to print is more important to becoming a* **COMPETENT** *reader than a* **KNOWLEDGE** *of phonics.*

'Sounding out' is difficult for beginning and discouraged readers.

To appreciate how hard it is to read by sounding out, I would like you to do the following activities. In a workshop some years ago, I was impressed by the way this exercise helped me put phonics and experience into perspective.

Read the following words. They are phonetically correct, but are spelled differently from the way you have learned them. You will find this assignment challenging but don't worry, so does everyone else!

vury	sctraugh
mould	sought
whoamb	phyue
dauss	ceokn
whir	pneocquez

Did you find it impossible, as I did, to read this list with certainty? If you feel frustrated, you may be experiencing the same emotions as your beginning reader when he is asked to *sound it out* or read words from word lists.

Each word has a number of different possibilities, doesn't it? For instance, is *sc* pronounced *sk* or *s*? Even if we could recall all the ways sounds are represented in print we would still not know which to use.

Here is a story about baby robins. It contains the words you have just attempted to read from the list. If you have trouble with a word, look away from it and use your *experience* to think of what word would make sense.

"I am working vury hard," said the robin. "I am looking for sctraugh to build my nest. I shall use some mould, too. I shall line it with sought grass. This will make a nice whoamb for my baby birds." So she made the nest in the old apple tree. In a phyue dauss there were three little eggs in the nest. Ceokn there whir three baby robins. They stretched their little pneocquez and cried, "Peep, peep, feed us!"

Still rather difficult? But you were probably able to figure out some of the words and with a couple of re-readings you may be able to read the whole passage. Your understanding of the subject helps to limit the possibilities. It makes it easier to decode the unfamiliar words.

Look at this sentence as an example: "I shall use some mould too." In my workshops, some of those who read this say the word that means *green fuzzy stuff on bread* and just keep on reading. But when I stop and ask, "Does that fit with your knowledge of robin's nests?" they soon change the word to *mud* which is what birds use to build nests.

When you have figured out the words from context, go back and read the word list. It is quite easy now, isn't it?

Which helped you the most in reading the passage, phonics or experience? Your experience with robins provided you with the understanding necessary to figure out the words.

Learning all the sounds and their combinations and trying to use them in words can be a difficult and frustrating task. As you experienced by working through this exercise, **too much** focus on phonics makes reading more difficult.

Another passage that I was given to read in a workshop also illustrates the role that experience plays in reading.

> The procedure is actually quite simple. First you arrange things into different groups. One pile may be sufficient depending on how much there is to do. It is important not to overdo things. That is, it is better to do too few things at one time than too many. In the short run, this may not seem important but complications can easily arise. A mistake can be expensive as well. At first, the whole procedure will seem complicated. Soon, however, it will become just another fact of life. After the procedure is completed, one arranges the materials into different groups again. Then they can be put into their appropriate places.

Did you have trouble reading this paragraph? Not likely. Did you understand what you read? Probably not. Why does it not make sense?

If I tell you that this paragraph is about doing laundry, you can read it with perfect understanding, can't you? Your brain now knows which *little world of experience* to call on to structure meaning.

How literate are you? Although I read widely and have attended university for seven years, I am still illiterate! I am illiterate in a great many printed texts – computer handbooks, electricians' guides, lawyers' textbooks, mechanics' manuals, geological manuscripts and medical journals, to name only a few.

Recently, I picked up a copy of a newspaper that was published for truckers who drive large transports across North America. I was surprised to find that I couldn't understand some of the articles. I am not acquainted with the *worlds of experience* necessary to make sense of what was being discussed. Furthermore, I couldn't read some of the words! I had not heard them spoken and I didn't know for sure what sounds the letters made or which syllable to accent.

We are only literate in material for which we have some frame of reference, some level of experience. To understand words we must understand the world in which the words are being used. This is fundamental to the ability to read.

Yet children are often expected to read whatever is presented to them even though their background of experience is more limited than ours. An example of this problem is standardized reading tests in which passages reflect different fields of knowledge and sometimes even different cultures. The results from such tests are often treated seriously and used as a basis for labelling and sorting children. No wonder some get stressed and discouraged!

CONSONANTS AND VOWELS

You may find reading the following passage a challenge at first, but I hope it will get easier as you go along.

This segment is taken from a book called *The Rainbow Goblins*. The Color Goblins are making plans to steal the Rainbow.

The Rainbow Goblins

The_ g_bl_ns c__ld h_rdly c_nt__n th__r _xc_t_m_nt. "S__n _ll th_ c_l__rs _f th_ R__nb_w w_ll b_ __rs," Y_ll_w gl__t_d.

W_'ll sn_tch _t _s _t r_s_s," s__d Gr__n, "wh_n th_ c_l__rs _r_ st_ll fr_sh _nd cr__my."

Not too hard? Now try this one:

```
_ _e  _o_ _i_ _   _ou_ _   _a_ _ _ _   _o_ _ai_   _ _ei_
e_ _i_e_e_ _.  "_oo_  _ll  _ _e  _o_o_ _ _   _f  _ _e  _ai_ _o_
_i_ _  _e  ou_ _,"  _e_ _o_   _ _oa_e_ .
```

Impossible? Right! The first passage contains only consonants and the second, vowels. These passages illustrate that the most important clues are in consonants. Consonants seem to be more consistent than vowels and beginners find them much easier to use.

You will notice that children use consonants when they begin to write with letters. They seem to have more difficulty isolating vowel sounds than consonant sounds. Vowels are often irregular and cause the most trouble when figuring out words. Isn't it fortunate that children can get on with reading before they have learned all the vowel rules and sounds!

Compare another sentence from *The Rainbow Goblins* represented in two different ways.

```
The_   gob_ _ _   swu_ _   thei_   lass_ _ _   ar_ _ _ _   and
ar_ _ _ _   and  hur_ _ _   th_ _   in_ _   the  sk_.
```

and

```
_ _e   _ _ _ _ins   _ _ _ng   _ _eir   _ _ _ _oos   _ _ _ _nd  and
_ _ _ _nd  and   _ _ _led   _ _em   _ _to  the   _ _y
```

The first passage is quite easy, isn't it? The second is impossible. The beginnings of words contain the most important phonetic clues. Sometimes you do not have to look at the whole word because the initial sound triggers a word to fit the context. You can quickly check the rest of the word and go on.

Poor readers are often inefficient because they have been taught to look too carefully at each word. I help students to break this habit. Slow reading results in poor comprehension because the reader is so focused on individual words that he forgets what came before and has to re-read. For these children, reading is not enjoyable and so they avoid the practice needed to improve.

Reading **does involve blending sounds together and sounding out,** but the goal is to identify words using as **few** letters as possible. Effective readers depend less and less on analyzing all the parts and use consonants to make sensible predictions.

READING WITHOUT FORMAL INSTRUCTION

We have learned a great deal about reading from the research carried out with children who have learned to read without any direct instruction, sometimes at very early ages. For these children, there were no rules that needed to be learned. This may also be the case for those who read early in grade one. They have not had time to learn all the rules. Those who read well go beyond rules. They use their understanding to make sense.

I have worked with young children who read adult novels, but have a limited ability to hear individual sounds within words and are unable to spell with much success. Nicholas is a bright boy who had great difficulty reading simple grade one material. His mother told me that in grade two he suddenly started to read *Star Trek* novels on his own. He came to me for tutoring in spelling. I asked, "How do you read? I know you don't sound out all the letters in a word because you don't know your short vowels and you have difficulty hearing some of the consonants."

Nicholas looked up at me with a twinkle in his eye and a big smile on his face and said, "I only look at the beginnings and the ends."

I hugged him! "You have discovered the secret of reading. Now I will teach you to hear the sounds you need to learn to spell!" How fortunate for Nicholas that he wasn't handicapped by too much phonics before he learned to read! This is especially good news in a society where we **expect** children to read before many of them can isolate sounds or memorize rules.

Summary of Key POINTS

We are only **LITERATE** *in material with which we have some level of* **EXPERIENCE.** • *Sounding out is not only* **DIFFICULT**, *it is often impossible.* • *The most important clues are in the* **CONSONANTS.** • *Too much focus on phonics* **COMPLICATES** *reading.* • *Efficient readers depend less and less on the* **SOUNDS** *within individual words.*

Spelling and SIGHT WORDS

*Spelling should never be **CONFUSED** with reading. Although there are ways in which reading and spelling **SUPPORT** each other, they are opposite **SKILLS**. Spelling translates sounds to **LETTERS**, reading turns letters into **SOUNDS**.*

Stimulate interest in words by playing with them.

Reading is a creative art that involves blending ideas, discovering information and drawing conclusions. Correct spelling cannot be creative. It is standard in form with no room for individual interpretation. It is difficult and inconsistent.

Reading and spelling should compliment each other. Children are fascinated by rhymes and jingles. They chant together as they skip. Refrains that are repeated in stories are quickly learned and imitated. Children like to play with words that rhyme. Spelling these words is a good way to begin learning phonics.

Phonics is the study of how letters combine to make speech sounds. Familiarity with letter groups such as *ing*, and *ight*, helps children to recognize words more quickly. Spelling lessons are ideal for teaching phonics. The combinations learned become part of the child's *pool of knowledge*. They are then recognized more quickly and easily during reading.

Through reading some people develop a sense for correctness that makes them good spellers. Others become excellent readers and never learn to spell well.

I want to caution parents not to get anxious about spelling too soon. Children go through a series of stages as they learn to spell just as they do learning to talk. Early emphasis on rules can be confusing. The reality is, English is a highly irregular language!

Confidence is needed for spelling just as much as it is for reading. An interest in books is critical to reading. An interest in words is basic to spelling. Talk informally to your child about words and how they are constructed. Spelling out names on cereal boxes when you are shopping and noticing signs while driving are examples of ways to draw attention to spelling and to have fun with words.

When stories come home from school, discuss the content but don't draw attention to spelling errors. Accept phonetic spelling, a child's best attempt to put down what he hears. Children first need to gain confidence in their ability to write interesting stories.

Being able to spell correctly is important. Your child will be better able to take advantage of spelling instruction in school if he develops confidence and a positive attitude toward spelling at home. Unless children are interested in words and in spelling them correctly they may not put out the effort required to become good spellers.

THE USE OF SIGHT WORDS

Beginning readers should not be given too many sight words to memorize out of context. It is a difficult task for some children to read words in isolation. Often words that are read easily in a story are not recognized on a word list. However, words that become familiar through repetition while reading will be easier to recognize by themselves.

A mother in one of my workshops expressed frustration with trying to teach her daughter to identify fifty *sight words*. She was expected to spell them, too! Lisa was in grade two and was not yet reading independently. Reading time became a struggle and Lisa didn't want to read with her mother anymore. The quality of their relationship, so important to confidence, was suffering.

If a child brings home word lists to memorize before he can read, use them to make up crazy stories or poems. Find the words in magazines and circle them with a marker. Put them on cards and play a game. Children learn very well through play.

Was and *saw* are examples of words that beginning readers often confuse. Most children mix them up at one time or another. They are often only a *real* problem for children focused on *sounding out*. A reader who is concentrating on meaning will stop when he says the wrong word. For example, *I was a cow* and *I saw a cow* are quite different. Is it important at this stage to be able to read *was* and *saw* out of context? I don't think so.

SOMETIMES IT'S OK TO BE WRONG

In the beginning, don't correct words that are wrong if they still make sense. An example is substituting *house* for *home*. You want to emphasize the message that reading is making sense. However, do not allow *wild guessing* - saying any old word just to keep going. When this happens, stop and say, "Does that make sense? Listen!" Repeat the sentence the way it was read. Ask the child why it does not make sense and then figure out the correct word together. Or, after the child has identified the error, just give the right word and carry on to maintain fluency.

One mother told me that her daughter said "doo-dat-da-doo-wa" for "I want a drink of water". The family accepted the approximation and gave her a drink. In a spirit of fun, they asked each other for water in the same way. Everyone praised her attempts to communicate. They gave her as much time as she needed to speak correctly. This same spirit of fun and support must be maintained while children learn to read and spell.

The following poem demonstrates the complexities of spelling and the difficulties of using phonics to decode words.

ENGLISH

I take it you already know
Of tough and bough and cough and dough?
Others may stumble, but not you
On hiccough, thorough, slough and through?
Well done! And now you wish perhaps,
To learn of less familiar traps.

Beware of heard, a dreadful word
That looks like beard and sounds like bird
And dead: it's said like bed, not bead -
For goodness sake, don't call it deed!
Watch out for meat, and great and threat,
(They rhyme with suite and straight and debt).
A moth is not a moth in mother
Nor both in bother, broth in brother.

And here is not a match for there,
And dear and fear for bear and pear,
And then there's dose and rose and lose -
Just look them up - and goose and choose,
And cork and work and card and ward,
And font and front and word and sword,
And do and go, and thwart and cart -
Come, come, I've hardly made a start!

A dreadful language? Why, man alive!
I'd learned to talk it when I was five,
And yet to write it, the more I tried,
I hadn't learned it at fifty-five.

Author Unknown

Summary of Key POINTS

Spelling and reading are **DIFFERENT** *skills.* • *Spelling correctly is* **IMPORTANT** *for older students.* • *Support your child's* **DEVELOPMENT** *as a* **SPELLER** *just as you did as a speaker.* • *Do not emphasize word lists until your child has some* **SUCCESS** *in reading.* • **PRACTICE** *words that are difficult by creating games to* **PLAY** *with them.*

Instructive
FEEDBACK

Your **EFFECTIVENESS** *as a reading guide is enhanced when* **FEEDBACK** *on a child's reading* **IDENTIFIES** *helpful strategies and behaviours.*

Responses should strengthen skills and build confidence.

Reading coaches sometimes focus too much on the text and on getting it *just right*. The emphasis should be on making sense. Treat errors lightly to keep meaning flowing. Use difficult passages as opportunities to teach and reinforce effective behaviours. Knowing that it is ok to make mistakes lets a reader relax and read more naturally.

STRATEGIES TO USE WHEN READING TOGETHER

The following are ways to support your reader, add variety to your sharing time and build reading skills.

Spend a lot of time reading out loud together, in chorus. Stay just a little behind to give your learner the first chance, but come in fairly quickly to keep the meaning flowing. You'll get used to this with practice. Sometimes, just whispering the beginning sound softly is the only cue that is necessary to trigger a word that makes sense. Stop on long words and demonstrate how to blend the consonants.

▭ In the beginning, always take turns reading pages, paragraphs or sentences. If the material is difficult, you might read a page and the child will read only a sentence. Choose some passages to re-read so that the child can take on more of the reading.

▭ Sometimes it is valuable to read aloud the entire book, page or paragraph **before** the child attempts it. Pause to explain new words and ideas. This builds background information. You will be surprised at how quickly readers become successful when they have an understanding of the message.

▭ When an error is made, it is often wise to wait until the end of the sentence before drawing attention to the mistake. A suitable comment would then be, "Did you understand that? It didn't make sense to me because I heard . . . . . Is that what you heard?" Figure out the word together and re-read the sentence. Discuss phonics as much as you like at this point because you have emphasized meaning first. When a reader begins to stop on his own because it doesn't make sense, you know he is making good progress.

▭ If a child is struggling with a word you know he has heard before, tell him to leave it out and finish the sentence. Re-read the sentence aloud leaving out the word. Often the right word will pop into his head. Emphasize reading with consonants and predicting from the letter or blend of letters at the beginning of a word. Be generous. Don't feel guilty about telling him the word if he is struggling. This is not a contest! It is important that fluency and confidence are maintained. If a word is unfamiliar, explain what it means.

▭ A sure way to build confidence is to help your reader master a bit of difficult material. Say, "I will read a paragraph and I want you tell me what it says. Then we'll read it together and figure out all the words you don't know. With a few practices, you will probably be able to read it by yourself even though it's pretty hard!"

▭ Pick a book you have already shared and ask your child to read it aloud to you while you are busy doing something else. Every time he needs a word, either pop over and give it to him or have him spell it for you. This is a great way to get independent reading started.

▭ It is helpful for beginners to know four consonant pairs that together make a different sound than each letter by itself.

ch th wh sh

It is difficult to make a prediction if your reader thinks the word starts with s instead of *sh*.

▭ These are two phonics rules that I find the most useful. Point them out when it is appropriate.

A silent e at the end of a word like take
or shine *makes the vowel say its own name.*

When two vowels are together as in chain, *the first one
says its own name and the second is silent.*

Make your reader aware of the fact that, although these rules are helpful, we can't always rely on them because there are many exceptions. Using consonants to make sense should still be the first approach.

▭ A fun way to practice other simple combinations such as *ing* or *ight* is to make up silly rhymes using as many rhyming words as possible. Or, use a colored marker to circle all the *ing* words on a page of a newspaper or a magazine. This is also an excellent way to practice recognition of individual letters if that is still a problem.

▭ Look for chances to catch your reader doing something *right*. Tell her about it. Positive feedback is a powerful reinforcer. It lets the reader know you are paying attention. It identifies the behaviors that promote effective reading. It fosters the kind of self-talk that enables a child to see her own success and to realize that she can do it on her own.

REPLACE "SOUND IT OUT"

- "Trouble with that word? Let's leave it out and finish the sentence. I bet it will pop into your head. Sometimes we don't know what word will make sense until we hear the rest of the sentence."

- "Let's put the beginning and ending sounds together," or, "That's a long word. We need to look at the middle consonants as well."

- "Look at me and tell me what word that starts with *sh* would make sense in this sentence. I'll repeat the sentence and you put in the word for me. *Shout!* See, you have to use your head **and** your eyes to read. Good work!"

- "That's a word that tells you how horses run. They *ga....* Yes, they gallop around the pasture."

- "This word is made of two other words which each has its own meaning. *Greenhouse* is a house for green plants."

- "We can't always depend on sounds being what we think they should be. *Ch* usually sounds like it does in *choo-choo* but in this word *chorus* it has a *k* sound so we have to look at the other letters in the word. We can use our heads to think of what would make sense or ask someone for help."

- "I'm going to cover this word and I'll bet, without even seeing it, you can tell me what it is when you read the sentence!"

- "**Good reading!** That's exactly what you should do. You're really getting the idea, aren't you."

FOCUS ON THE POSITIVE

- "I like the way you recognized that long word so quickly. How did you do it?"

- "I like the way you put the beginning, middle and end sounds together and said that word without sounding out each letter."

- "I like the way you stopped reading when that sentence didn't make sense."

- "I like the way you used the beginning sound to put in a word that fit."

- "I like the way you can tell me the meaning of new words by how they are used in the story."

- "I like the way you said that part. It sounded just like how Red Riding Hood would probably talk to the wolf."

- "I like the way you made a movie of the story in your head so you could retell it so well."

- "I like the book you brought home for us to share. I didn't know that eels always go back to the Sargasso Sea to spawn."

- "I like the way you take those Franklin books and read them by yourself after we have shared them. You really enjoy that series, don't you?"

- "I like the way you told the story of *Tom Thumb* to Grandpa. You must have really listened to the details when we read it."

It is important that the kind of responses and feedback illustrated in these charts be a part of reading right from the beginning. Regardless of the teaching methods employed at school, use these strategies when reading at home.

Children who fail to learn quickly are sometimes tested and labelled. Unfortunately, they often live up to the label they are given. Both their own self-talk and the names they are called by others reinforce the belief that they are not *normal*.

Children hate being singled out. They want to be accepted as part of the group. Making them feel different from others not only affects reading but it destroys the confidence they need to learn other things as well. Feeling inferior can lead to behaviour problems.

Those who fail to keep up with what is *normal* for their age are sometimes slotted into very structured programs based on phonics instruction. Worksheets and reading exercises are assigned. Drills are conducted on sounds and blends. Errors are pointed out on a regular basis. Discouragement is built into every wrong response.

This kind of teaching doesn't provide opportunities for students to take advantage of their unique experiences and learning styles. Those with difficulties don't always need more phonics. They often need reassurance that they are *normal*, confidence in their ability to learn in the same way as everyone else, good literature to read and a broad range of strategies to use.

The plight of Scarecrow in *The Wizard of Oz* is similar to that of many who struggle with reading. Scarecrow wanted a brain. He travelled to the Wizard expecting him to use his wizardry to replace the straw in his head. The Wizard knew there was no magic cure. He sent Scarecrow to kill the Wicked Witch, a task that would require all his skills. When his friends were under attack, Scarecrow thought of a plan that saved their lives. He went on to become the ruler of Emerald City. He found his brain by using it!

Young readers need to discover and use their abilities. **They do this best by reading, not by doing exercises about reading!**

Summary of Key POINTS

Feedback should **IDENTIFY** *the strategies you want your reader to use.* • *Take turns reading.*

• **EMPHASIZE** *reading with consonants and thinking about what will make sense.*

• *Talk about phonics casually when it seems* **APPROPRIATE** *as you are reading.* •

Enjoyment in reading is the first **PRIORITY**.

Choosing the RIGHT BOOK

When finding books to share, **SELECT** *with as much* **CARE** *as you do when you put* **FOOD** *into your grocery cart.*

When choosing books you are choosing food for the mind.

The books you select are very important. A book worthy of reading will be one that you, as an adult, can enjoy. You will find the art delightful, the characters loveable, the contents interesting, instructive or just plain fun!

A good rule of thumb is to choose books which reflect the fact that both the author and the illustrator have spent time creating the best product possible.

Learning is cooperative. One of the best ways to explore an idea together is through a book. The dialogue inspired by a book is as important as the book itself. A good book will stimulate enjoyable discussions. Children need to look at books as a source of pleasure.

It is important to own some cherished books, friends that can be revisited often. But you must also breeze through a large number of books, some of which will be rejected because they are too difficult or uninteresting. **Visits to a library are essential!**

I asked one mother if she took her six-year-old daughter to the library. She replied that they had lots of books at home. I'm sure they do, but our brains thrive on novelty and freshness. Fresh books are as important as fresh vegetables.

The students I work with usually don't want to read the same book twice. With some information books we read only a page or two each session, especially if they are difficult. Sometimes I pick a paragraph and we practice it a few times so that my reader can hear himself reading fluently.

Make available a constant supply of fresh books on a variety of interesting topics. Read easy books alternately with ones which require more concentration.

There are so many wonderful books available that you don't need to waste valuable time on ones that aren't satisfying. Pick books with expressive words and well-written sentences. There should also be a good balance of short and long words.

Look at the difficulty of the content. Beginning readers need to be familiar with most of the *ideas* contained in the passage. If there are too many new words that need to be explained, put it aside until later. Go through the book first and discuss the pictures to build background.

Beginners especially like repetition that forms patterns in stories and verses that rhyme. Don't forget to include some poetry books in your sharing!

Some reading programs would have you believe that illustrations give children too many clues and make reading easy. How ridiculous! Illustrations do not replace text! I am a firm believer in the value of exposing children to fine art and I love beautiful books. I choose books with attractive illustrations and well-written text for my readers. Take advantage of the amazingly beautiful fiction and non-fiction books available for young people today.

It is possible to discuss, even with very young children, the uniqueness of each artist's style or the different ways in which wolves, trees and children are depicted. Discussion based on illustrations builds the *little worlds of experience* so crucial to reading.

The amount of print on each page should be a consideration. Inexperienced readers are uneasy if the page has too much print. I like books that have a small amount of information about one thing on each page. With this format, we quickly arrive at something to discuss.

Choose books which interest you both. In the beginning, follow the child's interest. But remember - it is the adult's job to stretch the child's understanding by introducing new subjects for discussion. Children don't always have to read about dinosaurs, sports, trucks or other current fascinations. I find it exciting when both my reader and I learn something new and it is a delightful treat to discover books that let us laugh together. Engage in stimulating conversations around interesting books and together you will develop a relationship that will make practicing enjoyable.

CONTENT IS IMPORTANT

Texts that are based on a phonics approach to reading often have stories that don't make much sense. They read much like this:

This is a rug.

This is mud.

The rug is in the mud.

The mud is in the sun.

I hit the rug.

The rug is fun.

Is the rug in the mud?

Is the mud in the sun?

Is the rug fun?

In the early days of reading instruction in North America, the first reading text students encountered contained **real stories** with **interesting words and plots**. The subject matter was not chosen for simplicity or made up to practice phonics. A page from an old primer illustrates the worthwhile content and complex sentences that beginners were presented with in their **first reading book**.

The Phonics Primer, Alexander Reading Series, 1915.

Here is a spider. He is in his web. See how fat he is! He must have eaten a great many flies to make him so fat.

He spins a pretty round web, and then says, "Come, little fly, come into my web!"

But if the little fly is wise, he will not listen to the spider's sweet words, for he would never come out of the web again, and would soon be a little dead fly.

Children need real literature right from the start! In these early primers children were introduced to reading through stories that made sense. The content represented a familiar world. Words were chosen to communicate ideas, not to teach sounds.

Sometimes beginning readers are given the most difficult text to read – small words chosen to fit small people! Each word has to be decoded individually and the stories are so simple that they aren't worth the effort.

Big words are often more phonetically regular and easier to read than little words and they are certainly a lot more interesting. It's almost impossible to develop the habit of reading the consonants and using them to make sense when the words are all short and the message is meaningless.

You will be surprised at how beginning readers exceed your expectations when they read from understanding rather than from a focus on memorizing letter combinations and sounding out words.

When choosing books to share, include some difficult material. You are the coach. You are there to help. Many of the common words will be familiar to your reader. The tough words will provide opportunity to practice the strategies presented in this book.

Until he is able to read with some fluency, don't ask your child to read alone from books which have not already been shared. Young readers can quickly become discouraged. They can develop bad habits such as sounding out every letter and *wild guessing*.

When your child was learning to walk, you didn't let him struggle on his own and fall down. You provided support for as long as it was needed. Even after he became a competent walker, he still liked to hold your hand on a walk. So it is with reading. Continue to read with your young charges for as long as they need it and enjoy it!

The fondest memory I have from my school days is of the teacher reading from a chapter book every afternoon. Caught up in the excitement of the story, we would beg for *just one more* chapter. It was so difficult to wait until tomorrow!

Stories transported me from our small town on the prairies to the far corners of the earth. I became acquainted with pirates and kings. I visited Heidi in the mountains of Switzerland where we shared bread and cheese and fresh goat's milk. I can't bring myself to view the movie version. I don't want to erase the scenes still vivid in my imagination.

My uncle talks about his love for the tales of Peter Rabbit. He says he read them hundreds of times. He became a self-educated man through his devotion to reading. Peter Rabbit can take the credit!

My editor told me she had a big, old, illustrated dictionary when she was young. It had coloured pictures of fish and birds, etc. It was one of the best investments her parents ever made. Terry spent many hours moving from the illustrations to new words, on other pages. Her parents helped her with the tough words, but the important part was that she remembered the words she discovered on her own. She told the librarian she wanted to be a volcanologist when she grew up! As a college instructor, Terry still uses an illustrated dictionary and still likes volcanoes.

Loving even **one book** can influence a lifetime. Buy your children beautiful books. Take them to browse in the best bookstores in town. Some hardcover books will be expensive – but worth it! Excellent, inexpensive soft cover editions make books affordable for all.

The best educational investment you can make for your children is in books that they love and enjoy. Compare the amount of money you spend on reading material with your spending on toys, sports equipment and treats. How you choose to spend your money gives a message about what you value!

Taste in books is as distinctive as taste in food. Don't force children to finish books they don't like. This means that you should have a lot of books at hand. Visit the library regularly. While the child picks out books, mom and dad can find books for sharing time on subjects that interest them. Reading and talking together builds positive relationships. The information learned will enhance your child's *pool of knowledge*.

Summary of Key POINTS

The book you **CHOOSE** will make a difference.

• Library visits are **CRITICAL**. • Discussion based on illustrations builds **EXPERIENCE**. • Use books to **STIMULATE** interesting dialogue. • Small words are often more **DIFFICULT** to read than big words. • Don't ask a beginner to read **ALONE** at first. • Continue to read to children even after they have **LEARNED** to read. • **LOVING** one book can interest a child in books **FOREVER**.

Handling

FRUSTRATION

Turn your **FRUSTRATION** *into* **JOY**. *Plan fun* **ACTIVITIES** *around books to create* **EXCITEMENT** *about reading.*

To teach, we must explore and notice things together.

Life is busy and full of problems. When children are learning to read or are not reading successfully, we worry about their progress. If they are not reading by the end of grade one, worry can turn into despair. Young readers sense your disappointment and lack of confidence in their ability. They get discouraged and may be reluctant to read to you. The temptation is to lecture about the importance of reading or to punish them by restricting TV or play time. **Don't!**

This is a critical time in your child's educational career. Her view of herself as a reader is at stake. Avoid getting into a struggle or a shouting match over reading. Attitude and emotional health are more important to reading than anything else at this stage. She doesn't need reprimanding - she needs to discover the **fun** of books and reading.

Don't ask her to read to you at all for a while. Give her time to regain her confidence. She doesn't want to be embarrassed before her family. Increase the time spent reading **to** her and spend more time talking and creating things together.

I told one teacher about the book I was writing. She asked me to share this experience with my readers. When her own boy was in grade one he refused to read to her. She became frustrated. But she didn't want to do anything that might *turn him off* reading. She just continued to read to him and expanded their sharing to include newspapers, magazines, and a variety of other written material. She believed that he would come to reading in his own time.

Ryan began to read in grade two and was soon anxious to read to anyone who would listen! He had been given support at home and time to take advantage of instruction at school. Ryan is now a successful reader who loves to read.

Children don't need lectures about reading, they need to discover that it's enjoyable! The time set aside for reading should strengthen your relationship with your child. Your primary task is to provide encouragement and to transmit a love for reading.

Creating an environment in which your child feels free to take risks will reduce tension and frustration. When you are both relaxed and have enjoyed some activities together, reading will be more successful. He will be more willing to try when he is not worried about letting you down.

A confident reader is a reader who is permitted to make mistakes. Opportunity must be provided to explore, fail, adjust and recoup without criticism. Read together with good humour, respect for the reader and without regard to timetables.

Conversation is a most important learning tool. Talk, talk, talk with your child about things that you know, have read in books or are questioning yourself. If you both become interested in a subject, look for more information. Read highlights from this material aloud. Simpler books on the same subject can then be read more easily by your child.

For instance, choose a book that involves a scientific concept. Check the date of publication to see if it is current. Get an older or a newer book to find out if the information has changed. Take a trip to a science centre or a planetarium. Read a biography about one of your child's heroes to stimulate interest in books about famous people. Extend your reading to include a wide range of topics.

This cannot start too early! We tie together our experiences by reflecting on and combining ideas. Connect what you are reading to other books or to real life experiences. Think of people you know who are like the people or animals in a story. Be creative! Do everything you can to make reading interesting! You will be rewarded by the sparkle in your child's eyes.

Progress in reading is directly related to the time invested just as it is for swimming, hockey or knitting. But the world will not come to an end if you do not read with your child every day! If you are tired, out of sorts, in a hurry or just reading to cover a prescribed number of pages, don't! Have a snack. Lie down for a few minutes. Get in the right frame of mind to spend pleasurable time together. Whether reading time is five minutes or an hour, both of you should come away feeling successful.

A full day at school can be tiring and frustrating for children as well. Don't get in a rut. Sometimes, simply talk about a favourite book, make a picture, take a walk or do something else you both enjoy.

The choice of books becomes even more important if you and your child are struggling. Books like *Simon in the Moonlight* by Giles Tibo are excellent. The art is exquisite, the story is short and the words are strong and expressive. When the story becomes familiar to your child he will feel comfortable reading sentences and then entire pages by himself. Feeling successful instills the confidence needed to attempt longer stories.

Approach reading in a light-hearted, joyful manner with the same confidence and spirit of fun that you had when your child was learning to walk and talk. **Lighten up!** Five minutes of shared enjoyment is better than thirty minutes of, "Let's get this over with so we can get on with our day!"

IDEAS TO GET YOU STARTED

I have a wonderful collection of original books made by children. Creating a book and sharing it with others is one of the best ways I have found to generate interest in reluctant readers. I save cloth scraps, used gift wrap and greeting cards, anything that might be used for collages. Images from children's wallpaper books, available at your local hardware store, inspire ideas for stories. Wallpaper samples are especially good because you can make books quickly and have a large collection in a short time.

Encourage your child to develop different artistic styles by having available a variety of paints, pastels and other art supplies. They love to copy the styles of artists from their favourite books. Barbara Reid, Ted Harrison and Eric Carle are good examples. Making books is fun. Reading their own creations to others is a remarkable confidence booster!

Write your favourite family stories from both the past and present. Your child will love reading them. These can become increasingly complex as the child's skill grows. Make original books about some of the stories. A scrap book filled with these anecdotes will become a family treasure.

Use a tape recorder to introduce variety into your sharing time. When you have finished reading, the child can retell the story on tape using his own words. Or you can stop before the end of a story to let the child create his own ending. Print out taped material and use it for reading. This is a great way to get reluctant readers started.

Retelling is also a valuable way to strengthen comprehension skills. Children who learn to visualize and make pictures in their heads store information in long term memory more efficiently. Assume the roles of characters in the story you have just read. Create conversations they might have had. Be an object in the story, e.g. the forest or baby's chair in *Goldilocks* and tell the story from another point of view. Tape the new version and use it for reading material or as the text for another book!

My daughter's family went on a trip when their son, Sean, was quite young. When they returned, she sequenced the pictures in an album and left it on the coffee table for him to look at. It became a favourite and he still remembers the trip. He also developed a fascination for pictures and photo albums. Photos can serve as the illustrations for a book about your vacation.

HELPERS ARE NEEDED

Many of these activities need the support of an adult or older child. Have fun with them so that they don't become just another chore. Co-author the book so that it is a joint effort. You contribute whatever is needed to make a product that you can both be proud of. If it's not fun and the child doesn't buy into it, postpone the activity and come to it from another way on another day!

Reading is its own reward. Resist the temptation to give treats, money or bicycles for progress in reading. A reward not gained is seen as a failure. You are communicating a subtle message: If you would just try harder you could do it. The child may already be giving his best effort. Your role is to provide encouragement!

CELEBRATING READING

If there is a tape available to accompany a book, have the child listen to it before you read together. After hearing the story, you will be surprised at how much of the text he can read by himself.

Ask your child to create a story based on the pictures in a book. You can tape it or just tell it for fun.

Teach your child how to ask good questions. Then have him question you about such things as the artist's style, the strengths and weaknesses of a story and so on.

Invite a friend (young or old) to bring a favourite book to share in your reading time.

In a special journal, make a *Books Shared Record*. Record the names of books shared, author, date and interesting comments. Many children love to copy so the entries might be done with a minimum of help. Include the books you read **to** the child in the Record.

▭ If you have grandparents or friends who are regular visitors, develop a routine where they look at new entries in the *Books Shared Record* and ask questions about any of the books listed. A sticker or signature can be used to indicate where to begin on the next visit.

▭ Have your child dictate or write a letter to someone telling about a book or an activity. He might write about the ways he sees himself improving as a reader.

▭ Help your child write a book for a younger sibling or a friend, telling them how to read. An original book would be a great gift for grandma and grandpa.

▭ If you have a video camera, create a documentary about reading. Tape a pretend interview with an author. Film an original play based on a favourite story. All members of the family can join in on the fun. Older kids especially like to do this. The video camera is an underused teaching tool!

▭ Use clay or play dough to create the setting and characters from one of your favourite stories. Make a cardboard backdrop and you will have a delightful display.

▭ Puppets are fun to use when telling a story. You could video tape your performance. Libraries have books on how to make both simple and complex puppets. Read them together!

Your child will build skills in many areas by engaging in these activities and you will discover many of your hidden talents, too!

A story is told about a woman who asked Einstein how to help her son excel in mathematics. Einstein told her to stretch his imagination and to teach him the great myths of the past. We must find ways to keep alive the creative imagination that is so evident in young children. Reading takes place in the imagination.

Summary of Key POINTS

Overcome frustration by creating **FUN** *activities.* • *Help children to* **EXPLORE** *and* **NOTICE** *things.* • *Resist putting too much pressure on beginners.* • *Above all else, make* **SHARING** *times* **ENJOYABLE**. • *Create a relaxed environment so that a child can take risks without fear of criticism.* • **CELEBRATE** *reading through enjoyable activities.* • *Let schools teach reading while you keep* **CONFIDENCE** *and* **DESIRE** *alive.* • *Reading is its own* **REWARD**!

Summary SUMMARY

The greatest **GIFT** *you can give your* **CHILD** *is a* **QUESTIONING** *mind that has been taught a variety of ways to find* **ANSWERS** *to life's* **CHALLENGES**.

Helping another to become a reader requires time, effort and patience.

No amount of force can open the door to another's mind. The key is on the inside.

We want children to feel successful so they can praise themselves and talk to themselves as readers. Minimizing the attention paid to mistakes and looking for opportunities to focus attention on successful performance will help achieve this goal. Whatever you do, protect their self-image. Help them to *save face*.

I emphasize again the essential role that experience, housed in each unique *pool of knowledge*, plays in reading. Children become more effective readers if, in the beginning, a minimum of direct phonics instruction is given.

Create a comfortable reading environment making it safe to take risks. Challenge your young reader with a variety of materials, stimulating a love for reading. Children who experience the joy of reading choose to spend time with books.

You may have serious concerns about your child's progress. You know better than anyone how your child is doing. If you sense a problem developing, keep in close contact with the teacher but do not discuss it with the child. Remember, if he picks up on your uncertainty and becomes discouraged, the teacher's job will be more difficult.

Society has shaped our attitudes about learning to read by treating reading as a **skill** to be taught to children when they go to school. I view reading as an **art**. Teaching and instruction are important to learning an art, but there are many subjective things that can only be learned by working beside an artist. Reading treated as a skill makes it a duty to be performed. Reading treated as an art makes it a pleasure to be enjoyed.

I have shared with you my understanding of reading and some of my experiences with young readers and their parents. I hope the view of reading presented in this book will make reading time with your child even more special and enjoyable.

A story is told of the great pianist Paderewski who was performing at Carnegie Hall. When Paderewski left the piano at intermission, a young boy climbed on the stage, sat down at the piano and began to play chopsticks. The audience was aghast at the young fellow's impudence. Paderewski turned around and came back to the piano. Sitting down beside the boy, he began to play chopsticks with him.

Combine your talents. Together you will create a better performance.

Bibliography BOOKLIST

Meek, M., (1982). *Learning to Read.* London: Bodley Head

Ulderico, G. (1994). *The Rainbow Goblins.* New York: Thames and Hudson

SAMPLES OF BOOKS TO SHARE

▭ This short list is presented to illustrate the criteria I have found useful in choosing books for early reading. They are selected for their excellent artistic representations and their use of expressive words that make the text interesting and not too simple.

Ahlberg, A., McNaughton, C. (1990). *Big Bad Pig.*
  London: Walker Books

Beginners love this book because it is short, easy to learn and funny. This type of book is one they can quickly learn to read to others with great fluency.

Amazing Worlds Series (1990). Toronto: Stoddart

Excellent books, even for beginners. Photos are fascinating, passages short and print is easy to read. Read a few passages at a time and return to these books often. Some of the titles: Frogs & Toads, Bats, Birds, Crocodiles, Poisonous Animals.

Bailey, L., Kassian, O. (1992). *Vanishing Animals of the World.*
  Richmond Hill: Scholastic

This is an excellent series. There is just one animal on each page. The text is difficult, but with a little practice it is amazing how quickly early readers can read it. There are three books currently available in the series.

Barrett, J. and R. (1989). *Animals Should Definitely Not Wear
  Clothing.* New York: Collier Macmillan

Just for the fun of it! Excellent for patterning if you want to create your own books. For example, Animals Should Definitely Not Attend Parties or Children Should Definitely. . . etc.

Bourgeois, P. & Clark, B. (1992). *The Franklin Series.*
    Toronto: Kids Can Press.

Deals very gently with behaviours such as lying, bossing others and being a poor sport. Children love Franklin. After a few readings you will be surprised at how well your beginner can read these fairly difficult books.

Burningham, J. (1993). *Aldo.* New York: Random House

Burningham's books have been a favourite with young children for many years. They have simple illustrations, large print and interesting stories. There are lots of titles at your library.

Eyewitness Books. (1990). Toronto: Stoddart

There are over forty books in this series on every subject from Sports to Egyptian Mummys. Each is a mini-museum with short paragraphs that are perfect for use during sharing time. This series is a must for both the beginner and the discouraged reader.

Harrison, T. (1992). *A Northern Alphabet and Children of the Yukon.*
    Montreal: Tundra Books

Harrison has a unique artistic style. His books have a northern native theme. They are excellent read-alouds. Use Harrison's art as a model for creating collages or paintings.

Hayes, S. (1993). *Nine Ducks Nine.* London: Walker

Repeats the refrain. A good example of a patterned book. Just plain fun. Look for the frog!

Jonas, A. (1989). *The Trek.* New York: Mulberry

This book is one in which you look for hidden objects. Young children love this kind of book.

Keats, E. *Over in the Meadow.* New York: Scholastic

An old rhyme beautifully illustrated by Ezra Jack Keats. Predictable rhythm and rhyme. Children enjoy making up their own verses. This poem can be found in other editions.

Lineker, G. (1994). *The Young Soccer Player.* Toronto: Stoddart

Well-illustrated book about soccer. Rules, skills, tactics are attractively presented. Reading and soccer will improve with this book!

Ling, M. (1992). *See How They Grow Series.* Richmond Hill: Scholastic

Books about the birth and early growth of animals and birds such as owls, kittens, rabbits and butterflies. These books are short, easy and well illustrated. Perfect for getting started.

Maestro, B. & G. *Take a Look at Snakes.* Richmond Hill: Scholastic

This is not a book to use at the very beginning. Extremely interesting, well illustrated, good sized print, not too much on each page. Choose a page or two at a session, not necessarily in order. Excellent for practicing big words in context.

Mayer, M. *What Do You Do With a Kangaroo?* New York: Scholastic

Mercer Mayer's books are excellent for beginners. A good example of an advanced patterned book. Use when your reader has gained skill and confidence. Copy the pattern to make your own original books.

McFarlane, B. (1990). *Hockey! The Book for Kids.* Toronto: Kids Can Press

Tips for kids on improving their game. Interesting stories about star players and great moments in hockey. Both you and your young hockey player will like this one!

McGovern, A. *Questions and Answers about Sharks.* Richmond Hill: Scholastic

A book for adults to read to children. Help the child read a sentence or two. He will read more and more each time it is shared until he can read it all.

Oppenheim, J., Reid, B. (1986). *Have you Seen Birds?*
Richmond Hill: Scholastic

Not for the very beginning reader, but excellent as a child becomes more skillful. Provides practice using phonics to read words in isolation with some support from the text. More effective than word lists!

Pope, J. (1988) *Kenneth Lilly's Animals - Wildlife Around the World.*
Boston: Candlewick Press

Superb book on animals. Text is difficult, but after reading and discussing it together you will be amazed at how your developing reader can read parts of it. Discuss long sentences together to build comprehension skills. A great book for practicing the reading behaviors presented in this book.

Scharer, N., Fitzgerald, J. (1992). *Emily's House.* Toronto: Groundwood

An excellent example of a book written in the cumulative style of the tale about the pig who wouldn't jump over the stile. Children who enjoy imitating animal sounds will love this one.

Tibo, G. (1991). *Simon series.* Montreal: Tundra

These books about Simon are my pick of the lot for beginning readers. The art is exquisite and the story outline is predictable. Spring, snowflakes, moonlight, feathers and birds are some of the topics that tie Simon's adventures to everyday happenings.

Waddell, M., Dale, P. (1992). *Once There Were Giants.* London: Walker

Warm, sympathetic depiction of the continuity of life. Good example of repetition used skillfully to enhance the story and to assist the beginner.

Wallace, K., Manning, M. (1995). *Read & Wonder Books.*
Cambridge: Candlewick Press

This excellent series about animals and nature does not attempt to control vocabulary, but is readable by young readers quite quickly. Nicely set up for turn-taking with one reader doing the story and the other reading the facts.

Other books in the Read and Wonder series:

All Pigs are Beautiful, A Piece of String is a Wonderful Thing, Think of an Eel, A Field Full of Horses, I Like Monkeys Because, Think of a Beaver.

Vera is available for speaking engagements and workshops. Parents and educators have found her presentations thought provoking and applicable to a wide variety of audiences.

"Vera's extensive experience and excellent personal and presentational skills make her welcome as a presenter to parents and community volunteers as well as to teacher and university audiences."

Dr. W.R. Dickson – *Deputy Chief Superintendent, Calgary Board of Education*

"Mrs. Goodman is truly a knowledgeable and entertaining presenter, a professional teacher who is familiar with the educational scene."

Stan Paulson – *Deputy Superintendent, Peace River School Division.*

"Vera has enlightened our parents with her substantial knowledge and expertise. Her humorous approach and genuine awareness make learning fun and give parents new confidence in themselves and in their children."

Gloria Deehan – *Parent Co-ordinator, Albert Park School*

To engage Vera as a speaker or to order further books, contact:

Reading Circles
P.O. Box 33038
3919 Richmond Road S.W.
Calgary, Alberta
Canada T3E 7E2

Phone or fax:
(403) 240-0402 OR 1-800-411-9660

Book Orders: Cdn. funds – **$12.95** plus GST / U.S. funds – **$9.95**

Add $2.00 for shipping and handling, plus $1.00 for each additional book. Please send a cheque or money order OR phone/fax credit card orders. Visa and MasterCard accepted.

Personal NOTES

Use these pages to make short, dated notes about your child's progress. Include your feelings about what is happening as you work together.

....

....

....

....

....

....

....

....

....

....

....

....

....

....

....

....

....

Personal NOTES

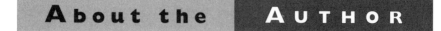

Jeremy and Kimberly enjoy reading a story with Vera.

Vera Goodman is an education consultant in Calgary with twenty-seven years of teaching and administrative experience in grades one to nine. She has shared her philosophy and innovative teaching practices with over two hundred audiences. She was an instructor with the Calgary Writing Project and chaired the first Young Writers' Conference, now an annual event in Calgary.

For years, Vera has provided support to anxious parents and frustrated children. She feels one of her greatest contributions in the field of literacy education has been to help parents understand the reading process. She hopes this book will serve as a coach's handbook.

Vera attended Moose Jaw Teachers' College and Seattle Pacific University. She has a master's degree in reading from the University of Calgary. Her thesis examined the roots of reading in book-sharing episodes with two-year-olds. It assessed the influence that a mother's hopes and expectations, routines, experiences and concepts of literacy have on a child's development. This may be the basis for her next book.

Vera lives in Calgary with her husband, Don. She has three daughters Cathy, Susan and Judy, a son-in-law Peter Blomfield and two grandsons, Sean and Bryce. When she isn't sharing a cup of tea with a friend, Vera likes to share the mountains with her horse, Missy.